THE WAY OF THE CHRISTIAN

ISBN 0 7175 0782 3

ACKNOWLEDGEMENTS

The author acknowledges with gratitude the helpful comments and advice received from the Rev. P. J. Edwards, the Rev. Canon and Mrs. P. Hawker, and the Rev. D. Pearce, C.R., during the preparation of this book.

We are indebted to the following for kindly allowing us to reproduce photographs:
The Mansell Collection; J. Allan Cash Ltd; The United Society for the Propagation of the Gospel; T. J. McNally; Peter Baker, A.R.P.S.; The Salvation Army; Roy Mackman Ltd. The author also supplied some photographs from his own collection.

Bible texts quoted are taken from *The New English Bible*, except where otherwise stated.

First published 1978 by
HULTON EDUCATIONAL PUBLICATIONS LTD
Raans Road, Amersham, Bucks.

Reprinted 1980, 1985

Printed in Hong Kong by Wing King Tong Co Ltd

THE WAY
OF THE
CHRISTIAN

JOHN CATLING ALLEN

HULTON EDUCATIONAL PUBLICATIONS

CONTENTS

The Holy Land . . . . *Page* 6

The Holy Bible 6

The Purpose of Life 8

The Problem of Evil 9

The Promise of a Saviour 10

The Jews 10

The Birth of Jesus 13

The Life and Teaching of Jesus 16

The Death and Resurrection of Jesus 28

The Holy Spirit 43

The Holy Trinity 44

The Early Church 46

Pope and Patriarchs 49

Monks and Monasteries 51

How the Church was Organised 53

Churches and Cathedrals 53

A Visit to an Ancient Church 55

Christianity in the Middle Ages .   .   .   .   . *page* 58

The Reformation   65

Christian Divisions   69

Christian Missions   70

Christian Worship   72

Christian Social Work   79

Christian Prayer   82

Life after Death   85

Index   87

The Holy Land

If you read the newspapers, you will find that some of them have weekly travel pages. There are articles on foreign countries, and also a number of travel advertisements. Among them you can sometimes see one entitled "The Journey of a Lifetime"—to the Holy Land. This small country in the Middle East is now called Israel. But until 1948, when the Jewish State of Israel was founded, it was called Palestine.

The Holy Land is not much larger than Wales. But it has always played a very important part in the history of the world. It is the land where two of the world's great religions began—Judaism and Christianity. It is also the land of the Bible where many of the historical events recorded in the Bible took place, and where much of it was written.

The Holy Bible

The Bible contains the sacred writings, or holy scriptures, of both Jews and Christians. It is the world's most treasured religious book, and is particularly important to Christians who often call it the Word of God. They believe that God speaks to people through this book revealing the truth about himself, and the way a Christian should live.

Strictly speaking, the Bible is not one book but a collection of books in one volume. In fact, the word "Bible" comes from the Greek word "Biblia", which means "Books". These books were written by different authors in Hebrew, Aramaic and Greek over a period of a thousand years—between the ninth century B.C. and the first century A.D. Their books are very different, and contain a wide variety of literature—history and folklore, laws and legends, poems and prayers, proverbs and prophecy, letters and sermons.

Although the books in the Bible are so varied, Christians believe that God guided and helped the writers to record his message to mankind. Christians, therefore, call the Bible an "inspired" book, and claim that it has divine authority.

The complete Bible has eighty books which are divided into three Sections—the Old Testament, the Apocrypha, and the New Testament.

The Old Testament has thirty nine books. They are the sacred writings of the Jewish people, but Christians also accept them as holy scripture. They were written between the ninth and fifth centuries B.C.

The Apocrypha—a Greek word meaning "secret" or "hidden"—has fourteen books. They are Jewish religious writings, and were written between the fourth century B.C. and the first century A.D. There has always been a difference of opinion amongst Christians as to whether they should be accepted as holy scripture. This is why they are included in some versions of the Bible, but not in others.

The New Testament has twenty seven books. They were written by Christians between the first and second centuries A.D., and all Christians accept them as holy scripture.

The word "Testament", which means "Covenant" or "Agreement", sums up the message of the Bible. For the Old and New Testaments give an account of the Agreements which God has made with his people.

The Purpose of Life

The Old Testament says, first of all, that the universe did not come into existence by chance, but was created by God. There are two different Creation stories at the beginning of the book Genesis (1-2: 4; 2: 5-23). But the authors do not attempt to give an accurate scientific account of creation. Their purpose in writing was not to describe *how* God created, but *why*.

Their stories reveal that God created the world for human beings, and that man is made "in the image and likeness of God" (Genesis 1: 26-27). This means that human beings not only have a body which will one day die, but also a soul which will live forever. It also means that God has given every human being the ability to think and choose and love.

The purpose for which people were made was summed up by a sixteenth-century Spanish soldier who became a Christian—St. Ignatius of Loyola. "God made us," he said, "to know him, to love him, and to serve him here on earth, and to be happy with him forever in heaven." But God's gift of free-will—the freedom to choose—means that he never forces anyone to obey him. God wants people to choose for themselves whether they will love and serve him or not.

The Problem of Evil

The story of Adam and Eve in the Garden of Eden (Genesis 2 and 3) tells us—in picture language—that human beings have chosen to live for themselves rather than for God. This means that everyone is born with a tendency to do evil as well as good.

The Bible does not tell us how evil began. Its origin is a mystery. But we do know that God is holy. He does not cause evil although he allows it to exist, and all down the ages men's minds have wrestled with the problem of evil. But the Bible makes it plain that evil can be overcome— by the supreme goodness and holiness of God.

The Promise of a Saviour

Christians believe that it was God's purpose to overcome evil by sending a Saviour—or deliverer—into the world. As St. Matthew's Gospel says, quoting the prophet Isaiah, "'Behold, a virgin shall conceive and bear a son, and his name shall be called Emmanuel' (which means, God with us)" (Matthew 1 : 23—R.S.V.). Isaiah also says, "For to us a child is born, to us a son is given; and the government will be upon his shoulder, and his name will be called 'Wonderful Counsellor, Mighty God, Everlasting Father, Prince of Peace'" (Isaiah 9: 6—R.S.V.).

The Jews

The Old Testament reveals how God prepared the world for the coming of the Saviour. Out of all the nations of the world, he chose one nation—the Israelites or Jews—to be his special people. He wanted to teach them to understand his ways because the Saviour was to be born as a Jew.

God began the long process of preparation for the Saviour's birth by making Agreements with two great men of faith—Abraham and Moses. He promised Abraham that his descendants would become a great

10

nation, and a blessing to the whole world (Genesis 12:2; 22:18). To Moses, God promised that he would remain faithful to his chosen people providing that they would remain faithful to him. God made this important promise at Mount Sinai after the Jews—led by Moses—had crossed the Red Sea and escaped from the bondage of slavery in Egypt. This great saving act of God—known as the Exodus—has always been remembered by the Jews, and at Mount Sinai they promised to remain faithful to God by keeping his commandments and obeying his laws (Exodus 19:5-6; 24:7-8).

But—in spite of all that God continued to do for them, and all that their religious leaders taught them—the Jews frequently refused to serve the one true God. When they broke God's commandments and disobeyed his laws, their prophets warned them that—if they did not serve the one true God—his judgement would fall upon them.

After suffering many national disasters, the Jews gradually learnt more about the character of God and his purpose for them. Prophets like Amos, Hosea, Isaiah, Jeremiah, and Ezekiel, taught them that God was good, loving and righteous, and wanted them to live particularly good lives because they were his special people. They were also taught that, one day, the promised Saviour would come to make a new Agreement with the whole human race.

God also prepared other nations for the coming of the Saviour so that, when the promised time came, the good

11

Virgin and Child by Raphael
(*The Sistine Madonna, Dresden*)

news could be spread throughout the world. So it was that the Greeks provided the world with a common language, and the Romans established universal peace throughout their great Empire.

The Birth of Jesus

The story of the Saviour's birth is to be found at the beginning of the Gospels of Matthew and Luke in the New Testament. These writers record that, when Palestine was occupied by the Romans, God chose a humble Jewish girl called Mary to be the mother of the Saviour.

Mary lived in the small town of Nazareth, and was a virgin engaged to a carpenter called Joseph. When she learnt that God wanted her to be the Saviour's mother, Mary wondered how this would be possible. But God made known to her that, if she agreed, she would conceive the Saviour by the direct action of God.

Mary agreed to God's plan. "I am the Lord's servant," she said. "As you have spoken, so be it" (Luke 1: 38). Joseph understood God's act, and married Mary in spite of the fact that she was pregnant.

Shortly before Mary was due to give birth to the Saviour, the Roman Emperor—Augustus Caesar—ordered a census of the population. Everyone had to go to his original home-town to register his name and be counted.

As Joseph was a descendant of the great Jewish King David, he had to go to Bethlehem, the city of David, to be registered with Mary his wife. When they arrived from Nazareth, the town was so crowded that the only accommodation they could find was in a stable. Here, the long-awaited Saviour was born. He might have been born in a grand palace or a great house. But God chose a simple stable for the Saviour's birth. He wanted him to share his life on earth with the poor, the homeless, and the outcasts of society.

Jesus the Christ

Mary named her son JESUS, which means SAVIOUR. He was also called CHRIST. This is not a name, but a title. It comes from the Greek word CHRISTOS, which is a translation of the Hebrew word MESSIAH meaning ANOINTED. Jesus was given this title because he was GOD'S ANOINTED, or Chosen One, sent to be a great prophet, priest and king, as well as Saviour.

Christians also refer to Jesus as OUR LORD, and call him the SON OF GOD because they believe that in Jesus God became man. This most important Christian belief is called the INCARNATION, which means "being made flesh". Christians therefore believe that Jesus is God as well as man.

St. John, at the beginning of his Gospel, expressed this belief in the following way. He calls Jesus the WORD OF GOD, and says, "When all things began, the Word already was. The Word dwelt with God, and what God was, the Word was . . . So the Word became flesh; he came to dwell among us" (John 1: 1-14).

B.C. and A.D.

The birth of Jesus was such an important event that the history of the world has been divided into two parts. The first part is called B.C.—BEFORE CHRIST—and the second part A.D. These letters stand for the Latin words ANNO DOMINI, which mean IN THE YEAR OF OUR LORD.

But the man who worked out this division made a mistake. He was a Christian monk called Dionysius who lived in Rome during the sixth century. He tried to work out the year in which Jesus was born from the Roman Calendar used in his day. But Dionysius made an error of about five years when he fixed the Christian Calendar to begin at A.D. 1. Jesus, in fact, was born about 5 B.C.—before the death of Herod the Great in 4 B.C.

Christmas and Epiphany

No one knows the exact date of the birth of Jesus. But Christians who live in Western countries celebrate his birthday on December 25th—*Christmas Day*. This is an important family festival for Christians. They rejoice and thank God for the birth of Jesus by attending special Church services, singing carols, exchanging presents, and holding parties.

Houses are gaily decorated for this festival, and many churches have a Christmas crib which is a model of the stable at Bethlehem. It contains statues of the baby Jesus lying in a manger, Mary and Joseph, the animals in the stable, and the shepherds who worshipped Jesus on the first Christmas night. The Wise Men, who came from the East to worship the new-born King, are often added later. Christians in the West celebrate this event on January 6th at a festival called *The Epiphany,* which means the "showing forth" of Jesus to the Gentiles, or non-Jews.

The Life and Teaching of Jesus

His Early Years

Jesus was brought up at Nazareth, a small town in the hills of Galilee. Little is known about the first thirty years of his life. But he was brought up like any other Jewish boy. He went to school at the local synagogue—the Jewish place of worship—where he learned to read and write, and was taught the Jewish religion. On Saturdays—the Jewish sabbath, or holy day—he also went to the synagogue with Mary and Joseph to take part in the weekly act of Jewish public worship.

When he was twelve, Jesus went to Jerusalem for the first time. He was taken by Joseph and Mary to celebrate the Feast of the Passover at the great Temple where the Jews worshipped God on important religious festivals.

16

(Top): View of Nazareth where Jesus grew up
(Bottom): The River Jordan showing the traditional
site of the baptism of Jesus

For, like all Jews over the age of twelve, Jesus now had to worship at the Temple at least once a year.

John the Baptist

Like Joseph, Jesus later became a carpenter. But when he was about thirty he began his mission of preaching and teaching the people about God. His cousin, John the Baptist, had already been called by God to prepare the way for him.

John preached to the Jews by the river Jordan, and large crowds flocked to hear him. He told them that the expected Saviour would soon appear, and urged them to give up their evil ways. Many who listened to John were sorry for the wrong things they had done. When they had confessed their sins, John baptised the people by plunging them beneath the waters of the river. This was a sign that their sins were to be washed away. Jesus, too, asked John to baptise him because he wanted to show the people that he was the promised Saviour.

His Temptations

After his baptism, Jesus began to prepare for his mission by going into the desert for forty days to be alone with God, and to pray. During this time he went without food, and was tempted to do God's work in ways which appeared to be easy; in fact, they were wrong. But Jesus realised that God's way was the way of love and suffering.

Christians remember the fasting and temptations of

Jesus during the forty days of *Lent*, which is the Christian season of fasting and self-denial.

His Ministry and Preaching

According to the writers of the four Gospels in the New Testament—Matthew, Mark, Luke and John—the public ministry of Jesus lasted between two and three years. Jesus spent much of this time preaching, teaching, and healing the sick in the district of Galilee where most of the people of Palestine lived.

Wherever he went, Jesus preached the Gospel. This word means GOOD NEWS—the good news of God's love for all men, and his forgiveness to those who turn to him in sorrow for their sins.

The people flocked to listen to Jesus. He taught them whenever they gathered round him—in their homes and in the streets, on the hillsides and by the Sea of Galilee, as well as in the synagogues and at the Temple in Jerusalem.

The people liked listening to Jesus because he was such a wonderful teacher. He spoke to them simply—in ways they could understand—and often told them short stories called PARABLES, which means COMPARISONS. Jesus compared God's love, care and compassion for them with things they knew about in their ordinary, everyday life.

The Twelve Apostles

Many of those who listened to the teaching of Jesus became his followers, or disciples. From them Jesus chose twelve men to be his apostles, or messengers. He gave them special training because he wanted them to help him preach the message of the Gospel.

Eleven of the apostles came from the district of Galilee, and four—Peter and Andrew, James and John—were fishermen on the Sea of Galilee. The twelfth apostle, Judas Iscariot, was the "odd man out" because he came from the district of Judea, and not from Galilee. Amongst the twelve, Jesus had three special friends—Peter, James and John—who helped him most of all.

The Kingdom of God

During his ministry Jesus often spoke about the Kingdom of God which he had come to establish on earth. This kingdom, unlike the kingdoms of the world, is not a kingdom of force and power. It is the kingdom of God's justice, love and peace, and is made up of those in every nation who accept God as the ruler of their lives.

Jesus urged everyone to enter the Kingdom of God so that God's will could be done on earth as it is in heaven. But Jesus taught that there is only one way to enter it. People must give up their evil ways, turn to God, and be humble, like little children. "I tell you," he said, "whoever does not accept the Kingdom of God like a child will never enter it" (Mark 10: 15).

Jesus explained the meaning of the Kingdom of God in parables, comparing it with things people knew about. He said that it is like the small mustard seed which grows taller than any other plant. So the Kingdom of God begins in a small way, but gradually grows bigger as more and more people accept God as the ruler of their lives.

In another parable Jesus said that it is like the hidden yeast in a loaf of bread. So the Kingdom of God is a hidden, but powerful, influence in the world.

Again, Jesus said that it is like a merchant looking for fine pearls. Finding one of great value, he sells all his possessions to buy it. So those who search for, and find, God's kingdom will willingly give up everything to enter it.

The Sermon on the Mount

If you read Chapters 5 to 7 in St. Matthew's Gospel, you will find an account of the teaching of Jesus on a number of important subjects. Although Bible scholars do not think that Jesus gave all this teaching on one particular occasion, it is called his "Sermon on the Mount".

Jesus began by telling his disciples that those who followed his teaching would be blest.

"How blest are those who know their need of God," he said; "the kingdom of heaven is theirs.

How blest are the sorrowful; they shall find consolation.

How blest are those of a gentle spirit; they shall have the earth for their possession.

How blest are those who hunger and thirst to see right prevail; they shall be satisfied.

How blest are those who show mercy; mercy shall be shown to them.

How blest are those whose hearts are pure; they shall see God.

How blest are the peacemakers; God shall call them his sons.

How blest are those who have suffered persecution for the cause of right; the kingdom of heaven is theirs" (Matthew 5: 3-11).

These sayings are called THE BEATITUDES.

Jesus continued his Sermon by giving his disciples further new teaching. He taught them with an authority which they had not experienced before, and set new standards of behaviour which they had not heard before. For example, Jesus told them how they should treat other people.

"Give when you are asked to give," he said (5: 42).

"Love your enemies and pray for your persecutors" (5: 43).

"If you forgive others the wrongs they have done, your heavenly Father will also forgive you" (6: 14).

"Pass no judgement, and you will not be judged" (7: 1).

22

"Always treat others as you would like them to treat you" (7: 12).

Jesus also taught his disciples to put their trust in God, who would supply their material, as well as their spiritual, needs.

"Set your mind on God's kingdom and his justice before everything else," he said, "and all the rest will come to you as well. So do not be anxious about tomorrow" (6: 33-34).

Love

The teaching of Jesus is summed up in the word LOVE. When a young lawyer asked him, "Which commandment is first of all?" Jesus replied, "The first is . . . 'Love the Lord your God with all your heart, with all your soul, with all your mind, and with all your strength.' The second is this: 'Love your neighbour as yourself.' There is no other commandment greater than these" (Mark 12: 28-31).

The religion taught by Jesus, which is called Christianity, is based on these two commandments. The followers of Jesus Christ, who are called Christians, should therefore be loving people. They should love God, and love their neighbours as themselves. Jesus never said that this would be easy—or possible without God's help. So he taught his disciples to pray because prayer unites us with God and with one another.

Prayer

Jesus himself was a great man of prayer. The Gospels record that he often spent many hours listening and talking to God. After healing crowds of sick people in Capernaum, for example, Mark says, "Very early next morning he got up and went out. He went away to a lonely spot and remained there in prayer" (Mark 1: 35). Luke also records that, before he chose the twelve apostles, Jesus "went out one day into the hills to pray, and spent the night in prayer to God" (Luke 6: 12).

In the Sermon on the Mount, Jesus taught his disciples how to pray. "When you pray," he said, "go into a room by yourself, shut the door and pray to your Father who is there in the secret place; and your Father who sees what is secret will reward you" (Matthew 6: 6). In other words, Jesus was saying that it is necessary, normally, to pray in a quiet place—away from the noise and bustle of the world.

Jesus also taught that it is not necessary to say long prayers. Like the recorded prayers of Jesus, those of his disciples need only be short and simple. For Christians believe that prayer is offered to a God of love, who hears the sincere prayers of everyone—and answers them. But he does not always answer them in the way people would like. Jesus did not teach his disciples to pray, "My will be done," but "Thy will be done."

The model, or pattern, prayer which Jesus gave his disciples is called THE LORD'S PRAYER. "This is how

24

you should pray," Jesus said,

" 'Our Father in heaven,
thy name be hallowed;
thy kingdom come,
thy will be done,
on earth as in heaven.
Give us today our daily bread.
Forgive us the wrong we have done,
as we have forgiven those who have wronged us.
And do not bring us to the test,
but save us from the evil one' " (Matthew 6: 9-13).

This prayer teaches Christians to think of God first when they pray, the needs of other people second, and their own needs last of all.

His Miracles

Jesus not only preached the Good News of God's love, but also made it known by his deeds. As St. Peter said, "He went about doing good" (Acts 10: 38). He healed the sick, delivered those possessed by evil spirits, and raised the dead to life.

Jesus also showed his power over nature—by changing water into wine at a wedding reception, by stopping a storm on the Sea of Galilee, and by feeding over 5,000 people with five loaves and two fishes.

These and other wonderful works of Jesus are called MIRACLES. They were signs of God's kingdom and

25

The eastern shore of the Sea of Galilee—
a familiar scene to Jesus during his Ministry

power at work among men, and showed his rule over sickness, disease, and nature. They cannot be explained by natural causes. But Christians believe that Jesus was able to perform miracles because he had the power of God.

His Enemies

Jesus also made God's love known by forgiving people their sins. By doing this, Jesus showed again that he had the power and authority of God. For God alone can forgive sins. But the Jewish religious leaders refused to believe that Jesus was the Son of God—in spite of his divine teaching and wonderful miracles—and turned against

26

him. Whenever Jesus forgave sins, they were very angry and accused him of blasphemy because he claimed to be equal with God.

The religious leaders also criticised Jesus because he mixed with the outcasts of Jewish society, especially with people called "tax-gatherers and sinners" whom they particularly despised. They accused him, too, of breaking the Jewish religious laws, especially on the sabbath when Jews were not allowed to work. But Jesus often healed on the sabbath. The religious leaders then accused him of working on the sabbath and breaking the law.

Jesus often spoke out against the behaviour and teaching of the religious leaders. He called them hypocrites, or play-actors, because they did not practise what they preached. They were more concerned to keep man-made religious rules and regulations than to serve God and help other people. So Jesus once told them, "You are like tombs covered with whitewash; they look well from outside, but inside they are full of dead men's bones and all kinds of filth. So it is with you: outside you look like honest men, but inside you are brim-full of hypocrisy and crime" (Matthew 23: 27).

Eventually the religious leaders became so angry that they began to think of ways to kill Jesus. They knew this would be difficult because most people thought Jesus was a good man. Many said he was a prophet, and some believed him to be the promised Saviour. But the more popular Jesus became, the more the religious leaders hated him. They were jealous of his popularity, and afraid of his new teaching which threatened their beliefs and challenged their way of life.

The Death and Resurrection of Jesus

Jesus Foretells his Death and Resurrection

One day, when Jesus was with his apostles at a town called Caesarea Philippi in northern Palestine, he asked them if they realised who he was. Only Peter knew the answer. "You are the Messiah," he replied, "the Son of the living God" (Matthew 16: 17). Jesus then told them that his enemies, the Jewish religious leaders, were planning to kill him. He warned them that he would suffer and die in Jerusalem, but would be raised to life again three days later.

Jesus knew that he had to suffer and die by crucifixion on a cross to show the world the depth and extent of God's love for everyone. "There is no greater love than this," he said, "that a man should lay down his life for his friends" (John 15: 13).

As the Suffering Servant of God foretold by the prophet Isaiah, Jesus knew, too, that he had to suffer and die for the sins of the world. "God loved the world so much," the apostle John wrote later in his Gospel, "that he gave his only Son, that everyone who has faith in him may not die but have eternal life" (John 3: 16).

28

Six centuries earlier, in one of his poems about the Suffering Servant, Isaiah had written,

"On himself he bore our sufferings,
  our torments he endured . . .
He was pierced for our transgressions,
  tortured for our iniquities;
the chastisement he bore is health for us
and by his scourging we are healed.
We had all strayed like sheep,
  each of us had gone his own way;
but the Lord laid upon him
the guilt of us all" (Isaiah 53: 4-6).

Although Jesus told his apostles several times that he would die and rise again, they did not believe him. They expected Jesus to be a warrior Saviour, who would command a Jewish army and defeat the hated Romans. Then, they thought, Jesus would become King of the Jews and give them special positions of authority in his kingdom.

But—as Jesus had realised during his temptations in the desert—he could not fulfil his mission for God either by battle and bloodshed, or by setting up a kingdom based on force and power. It was God's will that he should overcome evil, and deliver people from its power, by dying and rising from the dead.

The Raising of Lazarus

During his ministry Jesus sometimes visited Jerusalem. He stayed in the nearby village of Bethany with two sisters—Mary and Martha—and their brother Lazarus.

One day, when Jesus was preaching near the river Jordan, he received a message from Mary and Martha. They asked him to visit their brother who was very ill. By the time Jesus reached Bethany Lazarus had died. But Jesus brought him back to life again.

When the religious leaders heard what Jesus had done, they were very worried. They held a special meeting to discuss the matter, and Caiaphas, the high priest, decided that Jesus must die. But there was a problem. Before Jesus could be killed his enemies had to arrest him. But they did not know where he was. For, after raising Lazarus from the dead, Jesus left Bethany and secretly went to a village some distance away. He wanted to prepare for the time when he could no longer escape arrest.

His Last Journey to Jerusalem

Meanwhile, the religious leaders waited to see if Jesus would come to Jerusalem for the Feast of the Passover. This important festival was held in the spring and lasted a week. It was the most sacred time in the Jewish year when the Jews remembered how Moses delivered their ancestors from slavery in Egypt. Every year thousands of pilgrims came from all over the world, as well as from all parts of

Palestine, to keep the Feast in the Holy City.

Jesus also went to Jerusalem with his apostles for the Passover. They arrived in Bethany six days before the Feast, and Jesus stayed with his friends Mary, Martha and Lazarus. Jesus knew that his enemies would arrest and kill him. But he also realised that the time had come for him to die.

When the news of his arrival reached the religious leaders, they were determined to arrest him. But, again, there was a problem. They dared not take Jesus during the daytime—when he was in Jerusalem surrounded by the crowds—in case there was a riot. And in the evenings he was with his friends at Bethany.

Suddenly their problem was solved. Judas Iscariot, one of the apostles, offered to deliver Jesus to them if they gave him money. The religious leaders were delighted, and agreed to pay the traitor thirty pieces of silver—the price of a slave. Judas then waited for a suitable opportunity to betray his Master.

The Last Supper

Jesus realised that Judas was planning to betray him. But he did not want him to complete his plans before the Passover Supper.

According to the Gospel writers—Matthew, Mark and Luke—this sacred meal was held that year on the Thursday evening of Passover week. Jesus wanted to be alone with his apostles on this important occasion. So

31

he secretly made arrangements for them to eat the Passover Supper at a friend's house in Jerusalem. Christians sometimes call this meal the Last Supper, because it was the last time Jesus ate with his apostles before his death.

During the Supper Jesus did something very important which his apostles never forgot. He took bread, blessed it, broke it, and gave it to his apostles. "Take this and eat;" he said, "this is my body." Jesus then took a cup of wine, blessed it, and gave it to the apostles. "Drink from it, all of you," he said. "For this is my blood, the blood of the Covenant, shed for many for the forgiveness of sins" (Matthew 26: 26-28).

Jesus knew that he would die on the Cross the next day, and wanted his apostles to understand the reason for his death. So, in this dramatic way, he showed them that he would shed his blood and give his life for the sins of the world. He also wanted them to know that his death would bring about a new relationship between God and men. Christians believe that—because Jesus died on the Cross for the whole world—everyone can now come to God, receive forgiveness for his sins, and enter God's family, which is called the Church.

The Church's Most Important Service

When they had shared the blessed bread and wine at the Last Supper, Jesus told his apostles to continue this sacred meal after his death. "Do this," he said, "as a memorial of me."

Christians have obeyed this command of Jesus ever since in a service called the Eucharist (a Greek word meaning Thanksgiving), the Mass, or Holy Communion. This is the only service which Jesus gave to his followers, and it has always been the chief act of Christian worship. Something of its meaning is summed up in the words of the hymn:

"And now, O Father, mindful of the love
　That bought us, once for all, on Calvary's Tree,
　And having with us him that pleads above,
　We here present, we here spread forth to thee
　That only Offering perfect in thine eyes,
　The one true, pure, immortal Sacrifice.

Look, Father, look on his anointed face,
　And only look on us as found in him;
　Look not on our misusings of thy grace,
　Our prayer so languid, and our faith so dim:
　For lo! between our sins and their reward
　We set the Passion of thy Son our Lord."

His Betrayal and Arrest

During the Last Supper Judas went out to betray his Master. He knew that Jesus and the other apostles would soon be going to a nearby garden called Gethsemane outside the City walls.

Jesus, knowing that he was about to be arrested, went there to pray. While the apostles slept, he prayed in agony. He asked his Father to save him from the suffering he faced. "Father," he said, "if it be thy will, take this cup away from me. Yet not my will but thine be done" (Luke 22: 42).

Then Judas arrived with soldiers from the Temple Guard sent by the religious leaders to arrest Jesus. They did not know him. But Judas betrayed his Master to them with an arranged sign—a kiss of friendship. Jesus freely gave himself up to the soldiers who bound him with ropes. Meanwhile, the apostles, afraid that they might also be arrested, left Jesus and ran away.

His Trial before the Jews

The soldiers took Jesus to the high priest's house where he was tried by Caiaphas and the Sanhedrin, the Jewish court of justice.

Jesus had six "trials" before he was finally condemned to death. Not one of them was legal—even by Jewish and Roman standards. But his enemies did not worry about giving Jesus a fair trial. They wanted him put to death quickly—before the sabbath began at sunset on Friday.

But they had to find a charge against Jesus which would enable them to sentence him to death. Several attempts were made without success. Then Caiaphas asked Jesus a question he was bound to answer under

34

Jewish Law. "Are you the Messiah, the Son of the Blessed One?" he said. "I am," Jesus replied. It was the answer Caiaphas wanted. Jesus had openly claimed to be the promised Saviour, which was blasphemy to those who refused to believe in him. As the Jewish penalty for the sin of blasphemy was death, Caiaphas said to the Sanhedrin, "You have heard the blasphemy. What is your opinion?" They all agreed that Jesus was guilty and should be put to death.

His Trial before Pilate

But there was still a problem. The Romans did not allow the Jews to put anyone to death. Only the Roman Governor, Pontius Pilate, could pass the death sentence. Pilate was in Jerusalem at this time. So the Jewish leaders took Jesus to him early on Friday morning and demanded that he should be condemned to death.

As Pilate did not judge religious offences, the Jewish leaders changed the charge against Jesus from blasphemy to one of treason against Rome. This was a political crime which Pilate could not ignore, especially when he heard that Jesus claimed to be a king—the King of the Jews. But, after questioning Jesus carefully, Pilate realised that he was claiming religious—not political—authority. He decided that Jesus was innocent, and made several attempts to release him. But each time the Jewish leaders objected. They were determined that Jesus should die, and had gathered a great crowd of Jews to support them.

35

The crowd, stirred up by their leaders, soon became a raging mob. "Away with him! Away with him! Crucify him!" they shouted (John 19: 15). Finally, Pilate gave in to their demand, and condemned Jesus to death—in spite of his innocence. Then he handed him over to soldiers to be crucified, which was the normal Roman method of executing criminals.

Like all condemned criminals, Jesus was flogged by Roman soldiers before being crucified. When they heard that he claimed to be a king, they also made fun of him. They put a scarlet cloak round his bleeding shoulders, a crown of thorns on his head, and a reed in his right hand for a sceptre. They hit him, spat upon him, and knelt before him shouting, "Hail, King of the Jews" (Mark 15: 18).

His Death

After his flogging, Jesus could hardly walk. But the soldiers led him through the streets of Jerusalem to a hill called Calvary outside the City walls. This was the place of execution where Jesus was nailed to a cross between two thieves, who were being crucified at the same time. Above his head, Pilate put a notice in three languages—Hebrew, Greek and Latin—which said, "Jesus of Nazareth, King of the Jews" (John 19: 19).

Jesus hung in agony on the cross for six hours—from nine o'clock in the morning until the afternoon. At the foot of the cross he saw his mother, Mary, and some of his friends. But only one of the apostles was there—John. Judas, who bitterly regretted betraying Jesus, had hanged himself, and the others were in hiding.

Jesus also saw the Roman soldiers gambling for his clothes, and heard the Jewish rulers mocking him. But he never complained, and prayed for his murderers. "Father, forgive them;" he said, "they do not know what they are doing" (Luke 23: 34).

Finally, just before he died, Jesus cried out in a loud voice, "It is accomplished" (John 19:30). It was a triumphant shout of victory. For Jesus had completed the work which his Father had sent him to do. He had offered the perfect sacrifice of his sinless life for the sins of the world.

The Cross

Christians call the day on which Jesus died *Good Friday*. Many people cannot understand this because Jesus was such a good man, and never did anything wrong. He did not deserve to be put to death, and yet he was killed in a most cruel way. But Christians believe that Jesus died on the cross so that he could face the challenge of evil and overcome it with good.

Christians also believe that, by dying on the cross, Jesus has made it possible for everyone who believes in him to be delivered from the power of evil. As a simple Christian hymn says:

37

(Top) : The Crucifixion by Mantegna

(Bottom) : The Garden Tomb, Jerusalem. Jesus was buried in a rock-hewn tomb like this, from which he also rose from the dead.

"He died that we might be forgiven,
　He died to make us good;
　That we might go at last to heaven,
　Saved by his precious blood.

There was no other good enough
　To pay the price of sin;
　He only could unlock the gate
　Of heaven, and let us in."

The death of Jesus is of such importance to Christians that the cross is the chief symbol of their religion. Many ancient churches were built in the form of a cross, and nearly all churches have a cross on the altar or Communion table. Many Christians put crosses in their homes, and also make the sign of the cross when they pray.

His Burial

When Jesus was dead, two of his friends—Joseph of Arimathea and Nicodemus—took his body down from the cross. There was not time to complete the full Jewish burial preparations because the sabbath began at sunset on Friday when Jews were not allowed to work. But they wrapped the body in linen cloths, and buried Jesus in a new tomb cut out of the rock in a nearby garden. Then they placed a large rolling stone across the entrance to protect the tomb.

39

His Resurrection

Early on the following Sunday morning, when the sabbath was over, some women disciples of Jesus went to the tomb to complete the burial preparations. When they arrived, they were astonished. The large stone in front of the tomb had been rolled away, and the tomb was empty. They thought someone had stolen the body of Jesus, and hurried back to tell the apostles.

When the apostles heard the women's news, Peter and John immediately ran to the tomb. Peter went inside first, followed by John. They saw the linen cloths, which had been wrapped round the body, lying undisturbed. Then John realised what had happened. The body had not been stolen. Jesus had risen from the dead, as he had promised. He had conquered the power of suffering, sin and death, and was alive for evermore.

This mighty act of God is called the Resurrection. Christians believe that it was an event in history, and the greatest of all God's miracles, which proves the claim of Jesus to be the Son of God and Saviour of the world.

The good news of the resurrection of Jesus from the dead is the central message of the Christian Faith. For without the resurrection there would be no Christianity. As the great Christian missionary, St. Paul, later wrote, "If Christ was not raised, your faith has nothing in it and you are still in your old state of sin . . . But the truth is, Christ was raised to life—the first fruits of the harvest of the dead" (1 Corinthians 15: 17-20).

40

Easter

Christians celebrate the resurrection on *Easter Day*. This is the most important day in the Christian year when churches are especially well-attended, and beautifully decorated with spring flowers. Some churches also have an "Easter Garden". This is a model of the hill of Calvary with its three crosses, and the Garden of the Resurrection with its empty tomb.

Sunday

Christians also celebrate the resurrection every Sunday, which is often called the "Lord's Day". They keep Sunday as their weekly holy day because it was on the first day of the week that Jesus rose from the dead. It is the day when Christians gather together in churches for public worship, especially for the Eucharist. It is also a day of rest and recreation.

The Appearances of the Risen Lord

When Jesus died on Good Friday, his apostles were very sad. Their hopes that he was the promised Saviour were dashed, and they looked upon his death as a defeat. They certainly did not expect the resurrection—even though Jesus had promised to rise from the dead. So Jesus "showed himself to these men after his death, and gave them ample proof that he was alive: over a period of forty days he appeared to them and taught them about the kingdom of God" (Acts 1: 3). His appearances were

41

sudden and unexpected—at different times and in different places.

The apostles were not the kind of men who easily believed extraordinary events. But each time he appeared, Jesus made himself known to them. He not only spoke to them, but also answered their questions, and ate with them.

His Ascension

When the apostles were firmly convinced that he had risen from the dead, Jesus appeared to them for the last time—in Jerusalem. He led them out of the city to the Mount of Olives, and told them to continue his work. "Go forth therefore," he said, "and make all nations my disciples..." (Matthew 28: 19). They were to be witnesses of his resurrection, and spread the good news of God's love and God's kingdom throughout the world.

Jesus also told the apostles to remain in Jerusalem until they received special power from God to help them in their work. He promised to send them the gift of the Holy Spirit. "You will receive power," he said, "when the Holy Spirit comes upon you" (Acts 1: 8). Then Jesus blessed them, and they saw him no more. He had returned to his Father in heaven. Christians celebrate this event, which is called the Ascension, forty days after Easter on *Ascension Day*.

The Holy Spirit

After Jesus had ascended into heaven, the apostles remained in Jerusalem to wait for the coming of the Holy Spirit. Ten days later the Jews celebrated the Feast of Pentecost, which they kept in memory of the Law given to Moses on Mount Sinai. It was also the beginning of the harvest festival season, and Jerusalem was again crowded with pilgrims.

The apostles and other disciples were praying together in Jerusalem early on the day of Pentecost when, suddenly, the Holy Spirit of God came upon them. He breathed new life into them, filled them with power and strength, and brought about a great change in them all. They were no longer frightened, weak and cowardly people, but courageous, strong and brave.

The Birth of the Church

Immediately after they had received the gift of the Holy Spirit, the apostles went out into the streets of Jerusalem to tell people about Jesus. Crowds gathered to listen, and Peter preached his first sermon. He spoke about the death and resurrection of Jesus, and proclaimed him the Saviour of the world promised by the Old Testament prophets. Then he urged them to accept Jesus as their personal Lord and Saviour. "Repent," he said, "and be baptised, every one of you, in the name of Jesus the

Messiah for the forgiveness of your sins, and you will receive the gift of the Holy Spirit" (Acts 2: 38).

Peter's preaching was so effective that about 3000 people were baptised that day. So it was that—on the Jewish Feast of Pentecost in about the year A.D. 29—the Christian Church was born and began its work in the world, which has continued ever since.

In later years, Pentecost became a special day in the Church for baptisms. As those who were being baptised wore white clothes, it became known as "White Sunday", and then as *Whit Sunday*. It is the festival of the Holy Spirit, and the day when Christians celebrate the birth of the Church.

The Holy Trinity

The Sunday following Whit Sunday is called *Trinity Sunday*. This is another important day in the Christian Year when Christians celebrate their belief in God the Holy Trinity.

"Trinity" means Three-in-One, and Christians call God the Holy Trinity because they believe that there are "Three Persons in one God"—the Father, the Son (Jesus) and the Holy Spirit.

This does not mean that Christians believe in three gods. Like Jews and Muslims, they believe that there is only one God. But their belief about God is different from all

44

A missionary priest baptising an infant in Pakistan

other religions. They do not believe that he is an isolated individual Person, but a Fellowship of "Three Persons in one God".

This is a very difficult belief to understand. In fact, no human being can fully understand how God can be Three in One, or One in Three. But Christians believe that Jesus made known this truth about the nature of God.

The Early Church

The exciting story of the growth and spread of the early Church is told in the New Testament book "The Acts of the Apostles".

After Pentecost, the number of Jews who became Christians increased rapidly as a result of the apostles' preaching and healing miracles. They joined the other Christians in Jerusalem, and there was a wonderful sense of brotherhood amongst them. They shared their money and possessions, met together in houses for the Eucharist, and also continued their Jewish worship in the Temple and the synagogues.

But it was not long before the Jewish religious leaders became alarmed by the growing number of Christian converts. They did not expect to hear of Jesus again after his crucifixion. Yet his disciples were now openly claiming that he was alive, and healing people in his name.

So the religious leaders tried to stop them preaching. The apostles were arrested, put in prison, and beaten. But they continued to tell people about Jesus, and more and more Jews were converted.

Stephen

One of them was called Stephen, who became a deacon, or "helper", in the early Church. He was very brave, and spoke out against the Jewish religious leaders. So they accused him of blasphemy and stoned him to death. But, like Jesus, Stephen prayed for his murderers when he was dying. "Lord," he said, "do not hold this sin against them" (Acts 7: 60). He was the first Christian martyr to die for his faith in Jesus.

St. Paul

Among those who saw Stephen killed was a clever young Jewish Law student called Saul. He believed that the new religion of Christianity should be stamped out because it threatened the old beliefs of the Jews.

With the help of the Jewish religious leaders, Saul began a great persecution against the Christians in Jerusalem after Stephen's death. Many of them fled to other parts of Palestine, and some went to other countries. But wherever they went, they spoke about Jesus, and many more people became Christians. This made Saul so angry that he made plans to extend his persecution to Damascus in Syria. He intended to arrest the Christians there and bring them back to Jerusalem for trial.

But on his journey to Damascus Saul suddenly had a vision. He heard Jesus speaking to him. "Saul, Saul," he said, "why do you persecute me?" "Tell me, Lord, who you are," Saul asked. "I am Jesus whom you are persecuting," came the reply (Acts 9: 4-5). Saul later discovered that Jesus had appeared to him for a very special reason. He wanted him to spread the Christian message to people of all races in the Roman Empire— especially to the non-Jews, or Gentiles.

After his vision Saul became a Christian, and was baptised in Damascus. He was later called Paul, and became one of the greatest Christian missionaries the world has ever known. He made three long missionary journeys, and travelled throughout Asia Minor and Greece.

Wherever he went Paul preached the Good News about Jesus. He made numerous converts and founded many churches. He also wrote a number of important letters to Christians in Rome, Asia Minor and Greece, which are included in the New Testament.

During his Christian ministry Paul was often attacked and persecuted, especially by the Jews. The religious leaders particularly hated him, and wanted to kill him. Eventually, like Jesus, Paul was arrested in Jerusalem and falsely accused of crimes he had not committed. He was kept in prison for some time without a proper trial, and then appealed to be tried by the emperor in Rome.

The Persecution of Christians

By the time Paul arrived in Rome in about the year A.D. 60, Christianity had already reached the capital. When it continued to spread throughout the Roman Empire, the Roman authorities became alarmed. They were afraid of the growing power of the new religion, and believed that Christians were plotting against the State.

For more than three hundred years, many of the Roman emperors tried to stamp out Christianity by persecuting Christians. Vast numbers were killed, including St. Peter and St. Paul, and many of the Church's later leaders. But the courage and heroism of the Christian martyrs had such an effect on unbelievers that more and more of them became Christians. The result was that, in spite of centuries of persecution, the Church continued to grow stronger and stronger. As the great Christian teacher Tertullian said, "The blood of the martyrs is the seed of the Church."

Pope and Patriarchs

The persecutions ended during the reign of Constantine (306-337). He was the first Roman emperor to become a Christian, and his conversion marked a turning point in the history of the Church. For Constantine did all he could to help and support the work of the Church. Christianity then spread rapidly throughout the Roman world, and soon became the official religion of the Roman Empire.

By this time there were five chief bishops, or Patriarchs, in the Church—at Jerusalem, Antioch, Alexandria, Constantinople, and Rome. The Patriarch of Rome was thought to be particularly important because Rome was the capital of the Empire, and also the city where the apostles Peter and Paul died. He became known as the Pope, from a Latin word meaning Father, and later claimed to be the chief bishop of the whole Church. The four other Patriarchs, however, did not accept the Pope's claim, and would only recognise him as "first among equals".

When the Roman Empire was attacked by the barbarian Goths and Huns during the fourth and fifth centuries, it was divided into East and West. There were two emperors and two capitals—Rome in the West and Constantinople in the East. But in 476 the Western Empire collapsed as a result of the barbarian invasions, and the Church in the West became separated from the Church in the East. The Pope was recognised as the head of the western part of the Church. But in the East, which continued under the name of the Byzantine Empire until 1453, the Christians looked upon the Patriarch of Constantinople as their leader, especially when the Muslims—the followers of the new religion of Islam— conquered Jerusalem, Antioch, and Alexandria at the end of the seventh century.

Gradually, differences also developed in the worship and teaching of the eastern and western parts of the Church until finally, in 1054, they split apart. The Church in the West then became known as the Catholic Church, and the Church in the East as the Orthodox Church. The division between the two Churches continues to this day, and there are now a number of Orthodox Churches under different Patriarchs. But the Patriarch of Constantinople is still recognised as the most important. The largest of these Churches is the Russian Orthodox Church, which claims to have thirty million members—in spite of the persecution of Christians by the Communist regime.

Monks and Monasteries

From the early days of the Church some men believed that they could serve God best by living alone, apart from other people. They spent their lives praying and thinking about God, and were known as monks.

At first, they lived as hermits in huts or caves in the deserts of Egypt, Palestine and Syria. But before long groups of monks began to live together in monasteries. During the fourth century, St. Basil (330-379), Bishop of Caesarea, drew up rules suitable for monks living together, which are still followed by monks in the Eastern Orthodox Churches today.

51

One of the best-known early monks in the West was St. Benedict (480-550), who established monasteries which he called "Schools for God's Service". He drew up a new set of rules for his monks, which became the pattern for monasteries throughout Europe.

Like the monks in the East, St. Benedict's monks—the Benedictines—had to lead strict lives. Prayer was their main occupation, but they also had to work on the land, study the Scriptures, and help the poor. Like all monks, they also made three life-long vows—to live in poverty, to remain unmarried, and to obey their abbot, the "Father" of the monastery.

The influence of the monks was very great indeed. During the Dark Ages, when Europe was invaded and occupied by the barbarians, the monasteries were the only places where Christian civilisation survived. They became strongholds of Christian culture, learning and teaching. As well as cultivating the land, caring for the sick and poor, and giving hospitality to travellers, the monks also provided schools for boys. Above all, the monasteries were centres of Christian worship, prayer and missionary work. Most of the great missionaries in the next few centuries came from the monasteries, and it was largely as a result of their preaching and holy lives that Europe became Christian.

How the Church was Organised

When Christianity had spread throughout Europe, the Catholic Church in the West was organised in the same way as the Orthodox Churches in the East.

Countries were divided into areas called dioceses. Each diocese, which is also called a "See", was looked after by a bishop, who had his bishop's throne, or "cathedra", in the cathedral of his diocese. Later, the dioceses were grouped into provinces. In England there were two—a southern province under the Archbishop of Canterbury, and a northern province under the Archbishop of York.

Each diocese was also divided into smaller areas called parishes. Each parish had its own resident priest, who cared for the people and taught them the Christian Faith. Eventually each parish had its own church where the people—the parishioners—met for worship and prayer.

Churches and Cathedrals

During the Middle Ages, when everyone in the West belonged to the Catholic Church, beautiful churches and great cathedrals were built all over Europe for the

Tewkesbury Abbey, which combines Norman and
Gothic styles of architecture

worship and service of God. They show the strength of the Christian Faith, and the importance of Christian worship, at that time when the Church was the centre of people's lives.

The Normans were the first great church builders. After their conquest of England in 1066, they built solid churches and massive cathedrals throughout the country up to the end of the twelfth century. Then a new style of architecture was developed called Gothic, which covered three periods—Early English (thirteenth century), Decorated (fourteenth century), and Perpendicular (fifteenth century).

Britain has many ancient churches and cathedrals, but the Gothic type of church building is the most beautiful of all. The cathedrals and large churches took a long time to build, and include different styles of architecture. But they were usually built in the form of a cross facing east and, like all ancient churches, were divided into two main parts—the nave and the chancel.

A Visit to an Ancient Church

If you visit an ancient church, you will see that there is a tower at the west end. It contains bells which are rung before services calling the parishioners to the church for worship. Some churches also have tall slender spires pointing upwards to remind people of heaven.

One of the first things you will see when you go inside a church is the font. This is a large bowl standing on a stone column, which contains the water used when people are baptised. It stands near the door to remind Christians that baptism made them members of the Church.

The largest part of the church is the nave where the people sit. The two bays between the nave and the chancel give the building the form of a cross. One bay usually contains a Lady Chapel dedicated to the Virgin Mary, and the other a chapel dedicated to another saint.

The chancel is often divided from the nave by a screen. In some churches you can also still see the medieval rood-screen above it with carved figures of Jesus on the cross with the Virgin Mary and St. John on either side. (Rood is an old word for crucifix.)

Outside the chancel, on one side, is a lectern, or reading desk, with a large Bible which is read to the people during the services. On the other side is the pulpit which is used for preaching.

The chancel usually has two sections—the choir and the sanctuary. The choir contains seats for the clergy who conduct the services, and the choristers who lead the singing accompanied by the organ, which you will also see in the choir.

The sanctuary, which is separated from the choir by a rail, contains the main altar of the church. This is a large table of stone or wood used for the Church's most important service—the Eucharist, Mass, or Holy

56

Guildford Cathedral showing the Nave, Choir,
Sanctuary, and High Altar

Communion. A cross or crucifix stands on it with two or more candles on either side.

The altar, or Communion table, is the most prominent feature in every church, and the sanctuary surrounding it is usually very beautiful and often decorated with flowers. For it is here, at the altar rail, that Christians receive the blessed bread and wine in Holy Communion.

You will also see many other interesting and beautiful things in ancient churches—tombs, statues and shrines, as well as stained glass windows showing scenes from the Bible and pictures of the saints.

Christianity in the Middle Ages

The Middle Ages has been called an Age of Faith. For in those days, unlike today, the people had a strong belief in God and in a life after death. They did not doubt the reality of heaven and hell, angels and saints, the devil and demons.

They thought of heaven as a place of wonder and delight for good people, and hell as a place of suffering and torment for bad people. So they tried to lead good Christian lives by following the Church's teaching and obeying the Church's rules. For the Church taught that those who did not do so would go to hell.

The Church also taught that only those who lived exceptionally good lives—the saints—went direct to heaven. Other Christians went to a place called Purgatory where their souls were purged, or cleansed, from sin and made ready for heaven.

This belief led to the custom of priests offering Masses for the dead, and people left money in their wills for this purpose. Chantry chapels were also often built over the tombs of the wealthy where specially employed priests regularly said Masses for their souls.

The Saints

People also frequently asked the saints to pray for them. They especially prayed in front of statues of the Virgin Mary and other popular saints, which were to be found in every church surrounded by candles, lamps and flowers.

During the Christian Year the Church set aside certain days when particular saints were specially remembered. Like Sundays and other Holy Days, such as Christmas and Ascension, important Saints' Days were public holidays. On these occasions people always attended Mass at their parish church, and then met together for social activities. There was music and dancing, fun and feasting—especially on a Patronal Festival when the people honoured their Patron Saint, the Saint to whom their church was dedicated. Then, people from neighbouring parishes would join in the festivities, which often included either a fair, or a play telling the story of the Saint's life.

Pilgrimages

Sometimes people made long journeys, called pilgrimages, to visit Christian shrines and holy places. Wealthy people often went as far as the Holy Land. Others went to Rome to visit the tombs of St. Peter and St. Paul, and also to receive the Pope's blessing.

In England, many people went to Canterbury to visit the famous shrine of St. Thomas Becket, the Archbishop of Canterbury who was murdered in 1170 during the reign of Henry II. Another popular place of pilgrimage was the shrine of Our Lady (the Virgin Mary) at Walsingham in Norfolk, which was visited by pilgrims from all over Europe, as well as from all parts of England.

The Parish Priest

In the Middle Ages, when nearly everyone lived in villages or small towns, the parish church was the centre of people's lives. The parish priest, who looked after the church, was usually the most important person in the parish.

Like all the clergy in the Middle Ages, a parish priest was not allowed to marry. This Church law was intended to free him from family cares and concerns so that he could give himself entirely to God and his parishioners.

Although some clergy were very rich and worldly, most parish priests were very poor. But they usually lived

A priest saying Mass

good lives, and worked hard. For one of the few churchmen praised by Chaucer, the fourteenth-century poet—in his Prologue to *The Canterbury Tales*—was a poor parish priest who practised what he preached:

"But Christes lore, and his apostles twelve,
　He taughte, but first he folwed it him-selve."

The parish priest had many duties to perform. If he was a good priest, he cared for all his parishioners from the cradle to the grave. He knew everyone, and would visit them either on horseback or on foot. He helped the poor, looked after the needy, and ministered to the sick. Sometimes he also ran a small parish school, and taught the children to read and write. For, in those days, the priest might be the only educated person in the parish. The few other schools—for boys only—were usually attached to monasteries and cathedrals. But the parish priest's main work was to teach his people the Christian Faith and administer the Church's Sacraments.

The Sacraments

A Sacrament is a special sacred sign which brings God's help and strength to people. Catholic Christians believe that Jesus gave his Church seven Sacraments—Baptism, Confirmation, Confession, Communion, Marriage, Ordination and Anointing. (Protestant Christians recognise Baptism and Communion as "Sacraments of the Gospel", but not the other five.)

62

Like many priests today, the parish priest during the Middle Ages celebrated Communion, or Mass, every day. He baptised children, assured people of God's forgiveness after hearing their confessions, conducted weddings, and anointed the sick and dying with olive oil blessed by a bishop. He also had to see that baptised children were blessed and anointed with oil by a bishop in the Sacrament of Confirmation. For, like Ordination—the Sacrament which makes men bishops, priests and deacons—Confirmation can only be administered by a bishop.

Monks

The Church in the Middle Ages was served by a very large number of priests. Many were monks, but not all monks were priests. Every monastery had a large number of lay brothers, who did much of the hard work in the monastery and its grounds.

Many monks were Benedictines. Others belonged to newer religious orders. Among them was the large Cistercian Order, founded by St. Bernard in the twelfth century. The Cistercian monks farmed large areas of land in England and all over Europe, and their many hundred monasteries became very rich.

During the Crusades, when Christians were fighting the Muslim Turks in the Holy Land, special military orders of soldier-monks were founded to guard the Christian Holy Places, protect pilgrims, and minister to the sick and dying. The most famous were the Knights of

St. John and the Knights Templar, who became very influential and later moved to other lands.

Friars

At the beginning of the thirteenth century, St. Francis of Assisi in Italy, and St. Dominic, a Spanish priest, founded the Franciscan and Dominican Orders of Friars. Although they were very different from the earlier monks, they soon became very important.

Like the monks, the friars took three life-long vows— to live in poverty, to remain unmarried, and to obey their leaders. But instead of living in monasteries, they travelled about from place to place preaching to people in the streets and market places, as well as in churches.

The Franciscans, like St. Francis himself, were particularly poor, and lived very simply following the example of Jesus and his apostles. They not only preached, but also helped the poor, cared for lepers, and nursed the sick.

The Dominicans were scholars. They helped people to understand the Christian Faith more clearly, and trained new priests at the universities.

Nuns

As well as religious orders for men, there were also similar orders for women, who were called nuns. They took the same vows as monks and friars, and lived in convents.

Convents were run on the same lines as monasteries, but all nuns in the Middle Ages were strictly "enclosed". That is, they did not go out to work in the world, but spent their lives worshipping God, praying for other people, and working in their convents, as many nuns still do today.

The Reformation

By the end of the thirteenth century the Catholic Church was extremely strong and powerful. But during the fourteenth and fifteenth centuries its strength was gradually weakened by political, social and religious unrest, and its power declined. At the beginning of the sixteenth century the Church was in such a bad state that it urgently needed reforming.

Luther and Calvin

Then Martin Luther in Germany and John Calvin in Switzerland started a revolt against the teaching of the Catholic Church. This is known as the REFORMATION.

Luther and Calvin soon had many followers, who spread their teaching throughout Europe. They were called Protestants because they protested against the abuses and evils in the Church. Eventually they broke away from the Catholic Church, and formed separate Lutheran and Calvinist Protestant Churches.

Those who followed the teaching of Luther were called Lutherans. They belonged to the Lutheran Church which spread from Germany to Denmark, Norway and Sweden.

Those who followed the teaching of Calvin were called Calvinists. They belonged to the Reformed Church which spread from Switzerland to a number of other countries, including Scotland. Here, John Knox (1515-1572) established a strong Reformed Church known today as the Church of Scotland.

The Church of England

In England, the Reformation was different. Like the Lutheran and Calvinist Churches, the Church of England broke away from the Catholic Church on the Continent. But, unlike the Lutheran and Calvinist Churches, the Church of England kept much of its Catholic tradition. It not only stressed the importance of the Scriptures, the Creeds (the ancient statements of Christian belief), and the Sacraments, but also kept the ancient three-fold ministry of bishops, priests and deacons. So the Church of England, which is also known as the Anglican Church, followed the middle way of reform; it was both Catholic and Reformed—as it still is—and distinct from the new Protestant Churches.

In later centuries, when British colonies had been founded in many parts of the world, other Anglican Churches were established in such countries as America, Canada, Australia and New Zealand. But, unlike the

Church of England, they were free from all form of State control. Today, these independent self-governing Churches are called by different names. But they all belong to the world-wide Anglican Communion of Churches.

The English Protestants

Although many people were content to belong to the Church of England after its Reformation, some remained loyal to the Pope. They were called Roman Catholics. Others wanted to "purify" the Church of its Catholic beliefs and practices, and make it more like the Protestant Calvinist Churches. They were called Puritans.

During the sixteenth and seventeenth centuries there were bitter religious quarrels in England, and Roman Catholics and Puritans were often persecuted. Many were put in prison, some were killed, and others fled abroad. Eventually the Puritans left the Church of England. They formed separate Protestant Churches, and became either Congregationalists, Baptists or Quakers.

Later, in the eighteenth century, those who followed the teaching of John Wesley, an Anglican priest and famous preacher, also left the Church of England. They were called Methodists, and formed a separate Methodist Church, which had great influence amongst miners and factory workers during the Industrial Revolution in the nineteenth century.

The Roman Catholic Church

One of the important effects of the Protestant Reformation was that it led to a reforming movement in the Catholic Church, which is known as the Counter-Reformation.

It began in 1545 when the Pope and the Catholic bishops held a special Conference called the Council of Trent. The Council condemned all Protestant teaching, laid down the exact beliefs of the Catholic Church, and revised the Missal, or Mass book. But its main purpose was to correct the abuses and lax discipline in the Church so that it could fight back against the Protestants.

At the same time, new religious orders for men and women were established. Among them was the famous Society of Jesus, founded by Ignatius Loyola, a Spanish priest. Its members—the Jesuits—played a particularly important part in defending the Catholic religion against the attacks of the Protestant Reformers, and helped to check the spread of Protestantism.

Another well-known organisation which fought the spread of Protestantism in Catholic countries was the Inquisition, whose courts were greatly feared. For they had the power to try and condemn anyone suspected of heresy (wrong-thinking). Those found guilty were severely punished, and often burnt at the stake. But thousands of Protestants were prepared to die for their beliefs rather than give them up.

Christian Divisions

Although Jesus founded only one Church, and prayed that his followers would remain united, there have been differences of belief amongst Christians from the early days of the Church. But all Christians believe in Jesus Christ, and acknowledge him as the Son of God and the Saviour of the world. They differ in their beliefs on the authority of the Pope, the interpretation of scripture, and on the ministry and sacraments of the Church.

Only Roman Catholic Christians believe that the Pope is the supreme head of the Church on earth. Other Christians do not acknowledge the Pope's authority. But the Orthodox and Anglican Churches both claim to be Catholic in belief and practice. Protestant Christians follow the teachings of the different Protestant Reformers, and most of them have a different form of Christian Ministry from the ancient Catholic Churches.

Today, attempts are being made by all the main Christian Churches to recover the unity for which Jesus prayed. This hope is expressed in the Ecumenical Movement, in which the World Council of Churches and the Roman Catholic Secretariat for Promoting Christian Unity play an important part. Every year, in January, Christians throughout the world join together in a Week of Prayer for Christian Unity, and some Churches have already been united. In 1947, for example, several Churches joined together to form the Church of South India.

Christian Missions

Christianity is a missionary religion. For Jesus commanded his followers to spread the Christian message throughout the world. "Go forth," he said, "and make all nations my disciples" (Matthew 28 : 18). So, when Spanish and Portuguese explorers, like Christopher Columbus and Vasco da Gama, discovered new lands at the end of the fifteenth century, the Roman Catholic Church soon sent out missionaries to preach the Good News of God's love to people who had never heard of Jesus.

During the sixteenth and seventeenth centuries, Jesuits, Franciscans and Dominicans went from Europe to the West Indies and Mexico, South America and Canada in the West, as well as to India and the East Indies, Japan and China in the East. The most famous was Francis Xavier, a Spanish Jesuit, who has been called the greatest missionary since St. Paul. He converted thousands of people to Christianity in India and the Far East, and is known as "The Apostle of the Indies and Japan".

Among those who first introduced Christianity into North America were the English Puritan "Pilgrim

Fathers", who founded a colony in New England in 1620. Later, when other settlers established similar colonies, Christians gradually spread their beliefs throughout the North American Continent.

But it was not until the end of the eighteenth century that Anglican and Protestant missionaries went to other parts of the world. Then, members of the different Churches in England began to form missionary societies. They sent missionaries to many different countries—especially to India, Africa and China, and to the newly-discovered lands of Australia, New Zealand and the Pacific Islands. They were followed later by Roman Catholic and Protestant missionaries from Europe and America.

The result was that the nineteenth century saw the greatest expansion of Christianity in the whole of its history. But, as this great missionary movement took place when the European powers were extending their overseas colonies, Christianity was often associated with Western Imperialism.

Now that the colonial era has ended, the newly-independent countries do not always welcome missionaries from the West. So, in recent years, there has been a sharp decline in the number of missionaries working abroad. But Christianity is still spreading in many parts of the world—especially in Africa, Indonesia and South America—where strong and growing Churches have been established by the local Christian population.

71

Christian Worship

Jesus taught people to keep two great Commandments. "Love the Lord your God," he said, and "Love your neighbour as yourself" (Mark 12: 30-31).

Christians show their love for God first of all by worshipping him. This is their first and most important duty. For the word "worship" means "worth-ship", or acknowledging the worth of God. As the Book of Revelation says, "Our Lord and God! You are worthy to receive glory, honour, and power. For you created all things, and by your will they were given existence and life" (Revelation 4: 11—*Good News Bible*).

Christians meet together for worship in a church—especially on a Sunday, the Christian holy day, when morning and evening services are held in most churches.

The most important Christian service is the Holy Communion, which is usually called the Mass by Roman Catholics and the Eucharist by Anglicans. Protestants sometimes call it the Lord's Supper, or the Breaking of Bread. In Roman Catholic and Anglican churches it is held every Sunday, and often every day. In Protestant churches it may be held weekly, monthly or quarterly.

The form of the service varies in the different Christian Churches. But in recent years many Churches have introduced new Communion services which follow a

A priest giving Holy Communion to mixed races

similar pattern. Those used in Roman Catholic and Anglican Churches are most similar of all.

A Mass, Eucharist or Holy Communion Service

If you attend an Anglican Eucharist or a Roman Catholic Mass on a Sunday morning, you will see a number of sidesmen when you arrive at the church. They greet people at the door, give out prayer and hymn books, and show visitors to a seat. Men and women sit together, and there are mothers and fathers with their children, especially at a Parish Mass or Family Communion. When people get to their places, they kneel and pray in silence for a short while. Then they sit quietly until the service begins.

Most churches not only have an organist, but also a choir of men and boys—and sometimes women and girls, too. They are dressed in cassocks and white surplices, and lead the singing of the hymns and chants.

In the sanctuary there will probably be some servers— usually men or boys—who are often dressed like the choir. They assist the priest who conducts the service at the altar, which is usually lit with candles. He wears special clothes—either the traditional Mass vestments, or a white surplice and coloured stole—and often stands behind the altar facing the congregation. This helps the people to remember that they are the family of God worshipping together.

The first part of the service consists of prayers, lessons

from the Bible—usually read by members of the congregation—and a sermon, which may last from ten to fifteen minutes. The preacher will usually explain the meaning of one of the Bible readings, and show how it applies to the daily lives of the people. But sometimes he may preach a course of teaching sermons on the Christian Faith.

The second part of the service is the Communion when the priest repeats the actions and words of Jesus at the Last Supper. He takes bread and wine, which are often brought to the altar by members of the congregation. Meanwhile, during the singing of a hymn, the sidesmen

Choirboys singing at an open-air Eucharist, Capetown

take a collection, which the priest offers to God at the altar together with the bread and wine.

During the Prayer of Thanksgiving, the priest consecrates—or blesses—the bread and wine. Then he breaks the bread and gives Communion to the people, who leave their seats and either kneel or stand at the altar rail. Children, and others who have not been confirmed by a bishop, do not receive Communion. But they may be blessed by the priest. When the people return to their seats, they kneel and pray in silence until the service is concluded with a short prayer and a final hymn.

In many churches the people are invited to the church hall for tea or coffee after the service. This provides members of the congregation with an opportunity of getting to know each other better, and of welcoming visitors. For Christians believe that fellowship, or friendship, is very important in a Christian community.

A Protestant Service

If you attend a Protestant service on a Sunday morning, you will again be welcomed at the church door by a sidesman, who gives out hymn books but not prayer books.

When you enter the church, you will notice that it is different in many ways from an Anglican or Roman Catholic church. The pews or chairs in the main part of the building often have Bibles on them. But there are no kneelers because Protestants usually sit, rather than kneel, for prayer. At the far end of the church—in the centre—there is a pulpit or reading desk behind—or in front of—a plain Communion table without candles, and often no cross. But there may be either a large plain cross on the wall behind, or a verse from the Bible printed in large letters. Some churches have stained glass windows. But apart from flowers, which may surround the Communion table, there are no other decorations.

Some churches may hold their weekly, monthly or quarterly Communion service on a Sunday morning. But the usual service consists of hymns—often with rousing choruses—prayers, Bible readings, and a sermon. It is conducted from the pulpit or reading desk either by the minister, who often wears a plain black gown, or by a layman or laywoman dressed in ordinary clothes.

A large well-attended church has a mixed choir of men and women in plain dress, who will probably sing an anthem during the service while the congregation sits. A soloist may also sing a sacred song.

The prayers are said by the preacher. They are generally in his own words rather than prayers from a book. The sermon, which forms the climax of the service, is usually based on a verse or story from the Bible, and may last twenty minutes to half an hour.

Evening Services

In Protestant churches the Sunday evening service is often similar to the morning service. But sometimes—usually monthly or quarterly—it may be replaced or followed by the Lord's Supper when "all who love the Lord Jesus Christ" are generally invited to receive Communion.

Some churches also have a regular, or occasional, Guest or Mission Service when the Christian message is especially preached to people who do not normally attend a church. The preacher may urge them to repent of their sins, and give their lives to the Lord Jesus Christ. Those who respond may also be asked to leave their seats and go to the front of the church "to accept Jesus as their personal Lord and Saviour". After the service, they are helped to become practising Christians by the minister and other members of the congregation.

This type of service may also be held in some Anglican churches. But the usual Sunday evening service in an Anglican church is called Evening Prayer or Evensong. This follows a set pattern from a Prayer Book, and is made up of hymns, chants, prayers, Bible readings, and sermon. Sometimes, however, Evensong may be replaced by an evening Eucharist.

In Roman Catholic churches the Sunday evening service is nearly always a Mass. But sometimes there will be a service called Benediction in which the blessing is given with the consecrated Bread from the Mass.

Christian Social Work

The second of the two great Commandments which Jesus taught people to keep was "Love your neighbour as yourself" (Mark 12: 31). When a lawyer asked Jesus, "Who is my neighbour?" he replied by telling him the parable of the Good Samaritan (Luke 10: 25-37). This well-known story teaches Christians to care for other people, especially by giving practical help to those in need.

On many other occasions, too, Jesus taught his followers to show their love for God not only by worship and prayer, but also by loving and helping other people. For, as St. John says in his First Letter, "If a man says, 'I love God,' while hating his brother, he is a liar. If he does not love the brother whom he has seen, it cannot be that he loves God whom he has not seen. And indeed this command comes to us from Christ himself: that he who loves God must also love his brother" (1 John 4: 20-21). So Christians have always helped and cared for other people—particularly the sick, the poor and the needy.

Christians have also been involved in a great deal of social work from the earliest days of the Church. For they believe that the teaching of Jesus concerns people's social

A Salvation Army Officer feeding hungry children in India

and material well-being, as well as their individual and spiritual needs. Since the Industrial Revolution, for example, there have been many great Christian social reformers in Britain. They have fought against social evils, and worked for social justice to help people like the unemployed, the under-paid and the under-privileged.

Among them were William Wilberforce (1759-1833), who fought for the abolition of slavery; Lord Shaftesbury (1801-1885), who improved people's working conditions in factories, mills and mines; and Dr. Barnardo (1845-1905), who set up homes for homeless children and unwanted babies. Today, there are many "Dr.

Barnardo's Homes", and the work which he began is also now carried out by the Church of England Children's Society.

Christian women, too, have been great social workers and reformers. Among them were Elizabeth Fry (1780-1845), a Quaker, who worked for the improvement of conditions in prisons, and Florence Nightingale (1820-1910), who raised standards of nursing and improved conditions in hospitals.

Yet another famous Christian social worker was William Booth (1829-1912), who founded the Salvation Army, which is now a world-wide organisation and well-known for its practical Christian work. As well as providing homes for the homeless, the sick and the elderly, its members help all kinds of other people in need, such as alcoholics, drug addicts, and tramps. Later, in 1882, Wilson Carlile (1847-1942), an Anglican priest, founded the Church Army, which is run on the same lines as the Salvation Army. Its members, who belong to the Church of England, run hostels, homes and clubs for people in need, like the Salvation Army. But they also do mission work in parishes, and visit people in prison.

Today, the Welfare State has taken over much of the social work done by Christians in the past. But they still find many opportunities of helping people whose needs are not met by the social services. Christians, for example, are involved in the work of such well-known organisations as Alcoholics Anonymous, the Samaritans and

Shelter. They help the poor, the hungry and the homeless in the under-developed countries, too—by supporting organisations like Christian Aid, Oxfam and War on Want—and also work for social justice and human rights throughout the world.

Christian Prayer

Christians who practise their religion centre their lives on God. For they believe that man was made for God. As the great Christian teacher St. Augustine said in the fifth century, "God has made us for himself, and our hearts are restless until they find their rest in him." So, as well as joining in public worship and caring for other people, Christians also keep in personal touch with God by prayer, which St. Augustine described as "the turning of the heart to God".

Christians normally pray at least twice a day—in the morning and evening. Before speaking to God, they remember that he is present with them, and remain quiet for a few moments. When they talk to God, Christians use five different types of prayer. They adore, or praise, God; confess their sins and ask for his forgiveness; thank him for his great goodness and many blessings; pray for other people; and pray for themselves.

Sometimes Christians use prayers from a book. But very often they speak to God quite simply and naturally

Christians praying in a modern Church, Lincoln

in their own words. Some Christians—especially members of Pentecostal churches—also "speak in tongues" when they pray, like many of the early Christians. St. Paul wrote about this particular type of prayer in his First Letter to the Corinthians, Chapter 14.

But Christians do not only talk to God when they pray. They also listen to God speaking to them through the words of Holy Scripture. This type of prayer is called meditation. It helps Christians to know God better, love him more, and serve him more faithfully in their daily lives.

Many Christians meditate every day for twenty minutes or half an hour. They sometimes call this their "Quiet Time" with God. After praying for the guidance of God the Holy Spirit, they read slowly a short passage of Scripture—often from one of the four Gospels. Then they think about its meaning, and apply its teaching to their daily life. They may also express their love and affection for God in short acts of prayer and praise, or remain silent in the Presence of God. This type of prayer is known as the Prayer of Quiet, or Contemplation. It brings Christians into the closest union with God which is possible in this life.

In addition to their regular prayer times Christians often pray at other times as well, following the teaching of St. Paul, who said, "Pray continually" (1 Thessalonians 5:17). At mid-day, for example, many Christians say a prayer called the Angelus, or Angel's prayer, which reminds them of the birth of Jesus. They also thank God for their food by saying Grace before and after meals, and frequently say short prayers—known as "arrow prayers"—at other times during the day.

Like Jesus, who often went away to a quiet place to pray, Christians sometimes follow his example and also go away to pray for several days at a time. They go either to a monastery or convent, or to one of the many Retreat Houses up and down the country, where they can be quiet and pray in silence. This is called "going into Retreat".

Sometimes Christians go into Retreat on their own. But often they attend an organised Retreat conducted by a clergyman. Apart from the occasional talks which he gives, silence is kept throughout a Retreat, which may last two or three days, or even longer.

Life After Death

Christians, like other people, naturally mourn the loss of their relatives and friends when they die, and a Christian funeral is a solemn occasion. But it is not gloomy. For, unlike many people today, Christians do not believe that death is the end of life. On the contrary, they believe not only that a person's soul lives on after death, but also that those who have tried to do God's will here on earth will be happy with him forever in heaven. So the theme of a Christian funeral service is one of hope, and even joy, that the departed soul will enter into eternal life and rest in peace.

Christians also believe that at the Last Day Jesus will reveal himself in power and glory to judge all men. "Those who have done right will rise to life," he said; "those who have done wrong will rise to hear their doom" (John 5: 29). The New Testament teaches that, when this event takes place, every soul will be clothed with a new spiritual body. This is called the "resurrection of the dead".

St. Paul describes this Christian belief in 1 Corinthians, Chapter 15, and links it with belief in the resurrection of Jesus. "If there be no resurrection," he says, "then Christ was not raised; and if Christ was not raised, then our gospel is null and void, and so is your faith." But he goes on to say, "The truth is, Christ was raised to life . . . so in Christ all will be brought to life" (1 Corinthians 15: 13-22).

Christians, therefore, have a sure and certain hope of the resurrection to eternal life through Jesus Christ, and believe that life on earth is a preparation for life in heaven. But they do not believe that heaven is a place "above the bright blue sky", as many people think. They believe that it is a state in which all the faithful people of God are united with him and with one another, and in which they see God, as St. Paul says, "face to face" (1 Corinthians 13: 12).

Belief in a life after death is common to many religions. But Christianity differs in this respect from all other religions because it is founded not on speculation, but on the historical fact of the resurrection of Jesus. Christianity differs, too, from all other religions because it teaches that Jesus is the only way to God. "I am the way; I am the truth, and I am life," Jesus said; "no one comes to the Father except by me" (John 14: 6).

Index

Bible
Apocrypha; 7, 8
Books of; 7, 8
New Testament; 7, 8
Old Testament; 7, 8, 10

Church
Anglicans; 72
Baptists; 67
Benedictines; 52, 63
Bishops; 50, 63, 66, 68
Calvinists; 66
Cistercians; 63
Congregationalists; 67
Counter Reformation; 68
Council of Trent; 68
Creeds; 66
Crusades; 63
Deacons; 63, 66
Dioceses; 53
Divisions; 69
Dominicans; 64, 70
Ecumenical Movement; 69
Franciscans; 64, 70
Friars; 64
Inquisition; 68
Jesuits; 68, 70
Knights of St. John; 63, 64
Knights Templar; 64
Lutherans; 66
Methodists; 67
Ministry; 66, 69
Missionaries; 52, 70-71
Monks; 51-52; 63-64
Nuns; 64-65
Organisation of; 53
Parish Church; 53, 59, 60
Parishes; 53
Parish Priest; 53, 60, 62, 63
Parishioners; 53, 60
Patriarchs; 50, 51
Pope; 50, 60, 67; 68, 69
Priests; 59, 63, 64, 66
Protestants; 65, 68, 72, 76
Provinces; 53
Puritans; 67, 70

Quakers; 67
Reformation; 65-67
Roman Catholics; 67, 69, 72
Sacraments; 62-63; 66, 69
Saints; 58, 59
Society of Jesus; 68
World Council of Churches; 69

Church Buildings
Altar; 56, 58, 74
Architecture; 55
Bells; 55
Candles; 59, 74, 77
Cathedrals; 53, 55, 62
Chancel; 55, 56
Chantry Chapels; 59
Choir; 56, 77
Communion Table; 58, 77
Convents; 64, 65
Crib; 16
Crucifix; 58
Easter Garden; 41
Flowers; 58, 59, 77
Font; 56
Lady Chapel; 56
Lamps; 59
Lectern; 56
Monasteries; 51-52; 62, 63, 64, 65
Nave; 55, 56
Pulpit; 56, 77
Retreat Houses; 84
Rood Screen; 56
Sanctuary; 56, 58
Shrines; 58, 60
Spires; 55
Stained Glass Windows; 58, 77
Statues; 58, 59
Tombs; 58, 59, 60
Tower; 55

Churches
Anglican Church; 66
Anglican Churches; 66, 67, 69, 72, 74, 76, 78
Church of England; 66, 67
Church of Scotland; 66

INDEX

Church of South India; 70
Lutheran Church; 65, 66
Methodist Church; 67
Orthodox Churches; 51, 69
Pentecostal Churches; 83
Reformed Church; 66
Roman Catholic Church; 67-68; 70
Russian Orthodox Church; 51

Clothes
Cassocks; 74
Gown; 77
Stole; 74
Surplices; 74
Vestments; 74

Festivals and Holy Days
Ascension Day; 42
Christmas Day; 15
Easter Day; 41
Epiphany; 16
Good Friday; 37
Lent; 19
Patronal Festival; 59
Pentecost; 44
Saints' Days; 59
Sunday; 41, 72, 74, 76, 77
Trinity Sunday; 44
Whit Sunday; 44

God
Creator; 8-9
Holy Spirit; 43-44
Holy Trinity; 44-46
Worship of; 72-78

Jesus Christ
Apostles; 20
Arrest; 33
Ascension; 42
Baptism; 18
Betrayal; 33
Birth; 13-15
Burial; 39
Death; 36-37
Early Years; 16, 18
Enemies; 26-28; 30-31
Last Supper; 31-32
Miracles; 25-26; 30
Resurrection; 40

Resurrection Appearances; 41-42
Teaching; 19-25
Temptations; 18
Titles; 10, 14
Trials; 34-36

Life After Death
Death; 85
Heaven; 9, 55, 58, 59, 85, 86
Hell; 58
Judgement; 85
Last Day; 85
Purgatory; 59
Purpose of Life; 8, 9, 82
Resurrection of Dead; 85

Prayer
Angelus; 84
Arrow Prayers; 84
Contemplation; 84
Grace; 84
Lord's Prayer; 24, 25
Meditation; 83, 84
Prayer of Quiet; 84
Retreats; 84
Sign of Cross; 39
Speaking in Tongues; 83

Sacraments and Services
Anointing; 62, 63
Baptism; 18, 56, 62
Benediction; 78
Breaking of Bread; 72
Choir; 74
Confession; 62, 63
Confirmation; 62, 63
Eucharist; 33, 56, 72, 74, 78
Evensong; 78
Funeral; 85
Holy Communion; 33, 56, 57, 62, 63, 72, 75, 76, 77, 78
Lord's Supper; 72, 78
Marriage; 62
Mass; 33, 56, 59, 63, 72, 74, 78
Mission Service; 78
Ordination; 62, 63
Sermon; 75, 77, 78
Servers; 74
Sidesmen; 75, 76